AF259229

FAITH-BASED STRATEGIES TO PRODUCE MANIFESTATION OF YOUR GOALS

FAITH-BASED STRATEGIES TO PRODUCE MANIFESTATION OF YOUR GOALS

DENISE J. MEGGETT

ISBN-13: 978-1729713884

*Cover Design & Interior Formatting by
Cherese Agee, Rese Agee Media*

TABLE OF CONTENTS

INTRODUCTION

Faith-Based Strategies to Produce Manifestation of Your Goals is an opportunity for you to get focused and accomplish your goals. This book is designed to help you tap into the awesome potential that is awaiting you in your future.

How long have you wanted to purchase a house, get your degree, lose weight, relocate, seek that promotion, etc.? Have you obtained it yet? If so, praise God! If not, why not? You have to be real with yourself...brutally honest!

Ok, so how much longer are you going to allow your dreams to be held up because of YOU? Now, before you go into defense mode...think about it! How many excuses do you use to talk yourself out of pursuing what you want? I'm just asking...I'm praying for you because I want to see everyone win!

I developed this book as a tool to assist you because I believe we all can use a little push into our destiny. There is no better time than the present to become who you were created to be!

I believe you will unlock the door to the next level and I pray you will experience abundant joy along the way!

Faith is NOW – you have to move now! Therefore, as you start your journey to accomplishing your goals, realize that you must believe that you can and apply corresponding actions in order to see them come to pass.

Faith-Based Strategies to Produce Manifestation of Your Goals will only work if you work the steps. There's no magic spell or solution to you getting from point A to point B, but action! You must remain disciplined, consistent and focused as you embark on this journey to discovering all of the opportunities that await you.

ABOUT THE AUTHOR

MONCKS CORNER WIFE, mother, author, speaker, instructor, history enthusiast, traveler and music aficionada, Denise J. Meggett, has been a resident of South Carolina for 30 years. She was raised in Harlem, New York where she attended school before relocating to Edisto Island, South Carolina.

Meggett is a graduate of Trident Technical College and currently attends The University of South Carolina - The Palmetto College Chapter; where she plans to pursue a master's degree in English in the near future.

Meggett is currently an administrative coordinator with Trident Technical College at the main campus where she has also taught Continuing Education Courses. Meggett presently teaches several courses at a correctional facility several days a week such as public speaking, small business and Microsoft Word.

Being passionate about business, Meggett successfully owned & operated a Commercial Cleaning Company. Some of her former clients included several publicly traded companies such as Ryland Homes (now merged to form CalAtlantic Group, Inc.), Synovus (formerly NBSC Banks) and several small businesses.

She is the author of several self-published books, she loves writing poetry and is dedicated to her social media audience of nearly 5,000 as she shares empowering words with her enthusiast followers.

Meggett is the mother of three beautiful daughters whom she homeschooled for a few years until making the decision to place them in the Berkeley County School System to which she proudly celebrates their academic success having a recent college graduate of USC Aiken, along with a rising National Society of High School Scholars 12th grader and a high school sophomore who along with her sister attends Cane Bay High School.

STRATEGY #1 – ESTABLISH A PERSONAL RELATIONSHIP WITH GOD

NOTHING THAT WILL be successful and withstand the trials and difficulties of the world can be done without God.

You can do it without Him as so many do, but when trials or difficulties show up...you won't have peace or hope because you will only have yourself to rely on.

God will always be there and He will instruct you on ways to achieve your goals that man alone won't be able to do.

Since having a personal relationship with God (Jesus Christ), I've been able to see things so much clearer and grow in faith to believe for ANYTHING! The limits have been taken off because I know my Heavenly Father owns everything and loves me unconditionally. Therefore, I ask for what I desire according to His Will in order to be a blessing.

There is no greater love you can experience than the love of God! He is faithful to you, He is there to comfort you, He is your hiding place, He is a friend, He is your healer – I can go on and on! Developing a relationship with God is one of the best things I have ever done in my life and I wouldn't trade it for anything else.

Having a personal relationship with God is paramount in seeing your goals accomplished. Why struggle by yourself when you can have supernatural help? He will answer questions, grant you favor, open doors, provide resources–you just have to include Him in the process!

Write down your thoughts in the space provided. Here are some questions you may want to consider.

1. What are some ways that you will establish a personal relationship with God?

2. What testimony comes to mind when you think about the benefits of having a relationship with God?

3. What current goal are you struggling with accomplishing right now?

____

____

____

____

____

____

____

____

____

____

____

____

____

____

____

____

STRATEGY #2 – HAVE A TEACHABLE SPIRIT

LET'S SETTLE THE fact right now...You do NOT know everything! Ok, let that digest a bit. Now, since that is out of the way, you must have a teachable spirit - or be willing to listen, learn and apply information from a trusted source such as a Pastor, mentor, supervisor, spouse, parent, friend, etc.

Most people don't grow because they refuse to listen to others who have successfully accomplished what they themselves want to accomplish. This is where you have to mature and stop comparing yourself to them. You can't admire them secretly then hate on them publicly - that's doing nothing for your future.

Having a teachable spirit is key to your success. You need to find at least 2 - 3 people you can learn from, then listen to their advice or wisdom and then apply what you've learned once you've consulted God. Yes, God will place people in your life to help you get to the next level, but you have to trust Him.

I have been practicing this for YEARS! My mother taught me to always be ready to learn because you're never too old to receive new information. Therefore, I am able to evolve as God places the right people in my life. Two of my most cherished teachers are my Pastor Dr. Dexter Easley and First Lady Leisa. After 15 years with them, I am still learning and growing.

If you plan on seeing your goals manifest, you have to become humble and start speaking less and listening more...it's just that simple. Watch how your life will start to change!

Write down your thoughts in the space provided. Here are some questions you may want to consider.

1. Are you a manager or supervisor on your job? If so, is it hard for you to receive instructions?

2. Do you enjoy learning new things or is it challenging for you?

3. What are some ways you can challenge yourself to be a better listener?

____

____

____

____

____

____

____

____

____

____

____

____

____

STRATEGY #3 – BE PREPARED TO DO SOME HEART WORK SO HEALING CAN TAKE PLACE

IN ORDER FOR you to be in a position to successfully manifest your goals, you have to be whole! You CANNOT have unresolved issues, past hurt or sabotaging behavior that you are unwilling to deal with.

You may believe that wanting to lose weight or starting your own business is a solo project and has absolutely nothing to do with how you feel or how you behave with others. However, if you don't work on you; what's unresolved, hidden or broken in you will spill out to every segment of your life and produce unhealthy & temporary prototypes of success.

Have you ever seen people with a ton of money, yet they have horrible attitudes or are simply unhappy? Yes, they have some heart work that needs repairing, yet most people assume money or status can fix brokenness - it can't! In order to be whole, you have to confront your demons head on and be honest about them.

I used to suffer from low self-esteem for years because I was molested as a child and because I had the wrong self-image of who I was, I took on the responsibility of that situation. Well, by not dealing with the pain of my past, I developed sabotaging behaviors and gravitated to unhealthy relationships. It took me being brutally honest with myself and going to God to find healing.

I implore you to do the necessary work to be whole and free. Your future success will rest upon this indeed!

Write down your thoughts in the space provided. Here are some questions you may want to consider.

1. What are some difficult things that you know may be hindering your success?

2. Is talking about your past hard for you? If so, why?

3. In what way, can you begin to heal in one specific area of your life?

STRATEGY #3 – BE PREPARED TO DO SOME HEART WORK SO HEALING CAN TAKE PLACE

STRATEGY #4 – TRY NEW THINGS

EXPOSURE TO DIFFERENT cultures, people, systems, policies, hobbies, etc. can be enriching to your growth and vision.

In life, people tend to get stuck in a routine or traditional habit because it's comfortable. You can't grow if you're comfortable or if conditions are set to keep you doing the same thing.

Most people avoid meeting new people, trying new things or being uncomfortable because of fear of the unknown or because they cannot be in control of the situation - this is where trusting God is especially necessary.

Conquering my fear of the unknown was and still is important to me. Therefore, I do it regularly. I remember wanting to visit a friend in Atlanta a few years ago, but because I've never traveled by myself before, I was timid. So, I rented a vehicle, hopped in, found my playlist and locked the cruise control in place and I was off. I was so PROUD of myself. That experience opened the door and allowed my self-confidence to go into overdrive because I realized I was only limited by my false beliefs.

Be willing to step out there and trust the process of growth; knowing that God is with you. Don't allow you to be the reason why your goals never manifest...get out of your own way!

Write down your thoughts in the space provided. Here are some questions you may want to consider.

1. Does change scare you? If so, why?

2. What is the last thing you did that was new for you?

3. List (10) things you would like to try one day?

____

____

____

____

____

____

____

____

____

____

____

____

____

____

____

____

____

____

____

____

____

STRATEGY #5 – SEEK KNOWLEDGE, LEARN FROM OTHERS YOU ADMIRE AND ALLOW GOD TO LEAD YOU

AS YOU STRIVE to manifest your goals, you will need to be diligent about your growth. You cannot expect to obtain another level without the climb...this will take focus and effort.

Knowledge is vital in going forward on your journey to reaching your goals. Therefore, you will have to study the Word of God/The Bible. Yes, you can gain earthly knowledge as well...I'm an advocate for furthering your education; yet don't forsake God's knowledge and wisdom.

I also encourage you to start tapping into other sources around you. There are specific people that are in your life right now that were placed there to assist you in growing. Now, they may not look the way you expect or they may not be your favorite person, but pay attention to what they bring to the table. If their life is right and you see things in them that you truly admire...glean off of their experiences and know how.

God, too, is a direct source of knowledge! He will use a Scripture, people or a gentle nudge to direct you in this process. His instructions are the BEST because you know it will lead you to your goals. However, you have to work on developing that relationship we discussed in strategy #1 – that is why the order of these strategies worked so well in my life.

There's nothing that I can do without knowledge and

wisdom from God.

Deciding to seek knowledge is commendable, but remember you're not more important than anyone else remember you're not more important than anyone else because of what you know...it's a tool not a weapon!

Write down your thoughts in the space provided. Here are some questions you may want to consider.

1. In what ways can you learn more about your interest pertaining to your goals?

2. Who are some people that you can learn from about personal or business goals?

3. Do you believe you can learn from God? If so, in what ways?

____

____

____

____

____

____

____

____

____

____

____

____

STRATEGY #5 – SEEK KNOWLEDGE, LEARN FROM OTHERS YOU ADMIRE AND ALLOW GOD TO LEAD YOU

STRATEGY #6 – BE DISCIPLINED

OK, THIS IS not a favorite topic for many. However, this really is the lifeline to your success in life (besides Jesus). Those who achieve their goals - do it because they are disciplined.

So, you are trying to lose weight. Well, you already know the basics...eat better/healthy foods, exercise, drink more water, etc. However, that's the goal/plan. Discipline is the active ingredient to accomplishing your goals. You will have to not only plan, but create a schedule in order to actually complete each action step.

Once you have identified your action steps (detailed steps of what you need to do) then you should decide how much time you need to dedicate for each action step. Now, you have to apply discipline otherwise everything will simply remain on paper.

Becoming more disciplined will take help! You will need God to help you because you'll definitely have days when your attitude will be horrible (lol), you will need an accountability partner or focused friend and you will have to remain focused on your goals and not the temporary discomfort you'll experience.

You can do this...think about it! You get up to go to work...that takes discipline. You do many things throughout the day that requires discipline. Now, take it up a notch...you deserve this!

Write down your thoughts in the space provided. Here are some questions you may want to consider.

1. In what area are you most disciplined and least disciplined?

2. Do you have an accountability person who can assist you with being more disciplined?

3. Have you ever worked with a mentor? If so, what were the benefits?

____

____

____

____

____

____

____

____

____

____

____

____

____

____

____

____

____

____

STRATEGY #6 – BE DISCIPLINED

STRATEGY #7 – GET ORGANIZED

SO, BEING ORGANIZED is connected to becoming disciplined because it forces you to be accountable to an established system either created by yourself or outside forces.

Now, I have to say...this is my lane (well one of them). I thrive when things are orderly. It allows my creative energy to flow unhindered. I always encourage people to work towards being organized, especially when you have goals you'd like to see manifest.

You don't have to do this in one day or even a month. Set a short-term goal of 3 months and stick to it. Start with something small...if you need to get your closet organized, begin there. Create action steps (discussed in strategy #6). Ok, start with the shoes if that's the easiest then work toward the most complicated area. Make it fun - turn on your favorite music, put the phone away and don't stop until you're finished.

These strategies may sound elementary to you, but if you are not where you want to be and you're tired of struggling to get there; try them. I know first-hand these work. Now, I'm so not perfect; still a work in progress, but my life is orderly and I see the fruit from me sowing the right seeds in my garden.

Put in the necessary work to get to your destination. Don't keep saying you want it, but be unwilling to do what it takes. Organizing your life will prepare you to receive a greater harvest!

Write down your thoughts in the space provided. Here are some questions you may want to consider.

1. Are you an organized person? If no, why not?

2. Do you believe being organized is important? If so, why?

3. What is most challenging for you when it comes to staying organized?

____

____

____

____

____

____

____

____

____

____

____

____

____

____

____

____

____

____

STRATEGY #8 – WRITE YOUR GOALS DOWN ALONG WITH ACTION STEPS TO OBTAINING THEM

PURCHASE A NOTEBOOK/JOURNAL. I know we're in the digital age, but I'm old school. Writing down your goals or vision brings clarity and once perfected can be used for others to follow.

Dedicate your notebook to this purpose only. Be specific in your writings.

Vague: *I want to purchase a car.*
Specific: *I want to purchase a White xc90 Volvo debt free in 3 years.*

See the difference? You can't pursue goals you don't believe in or don't have the boldness to write/say. Start out with a priority list; listing your goals in order of importance.

1. Work on repairing credit report
2. Start saving money
3. Purchase property
4. Build house

Now, for each goal create action steps (detailed steps of what you need to do) which will help you accomplish them.

Your action steps should be practical, achievable and have a realistic timeframe. Don't write down something you know you can't or won't be able to do.

Goal: Working on repairing credit report

Action Steps...
• Order your free annual credit report.
• Dispute what's incorrect by writing letters to the company.
• Contact other companies to see if they'll accept a payoff amount.
• Start paying bills on time and set up bills to be drafted automatically.

Practical, achievable with a realistic timeframe.

You are the CEO of your life...God can't bless what you won't put your hands on. Therefore, a relationship alone with God won't manifest your goals, you must actively participate in your success!

Write down your thoughts in the space provided. Here are some questions you may want to consider.

1. Do you currently write things down? If not, why not?

2. Is it hard for you to remain committed to your plans? If so, why?

3. What are some ways you can reward yourself for accomplishing a goal?

STRATEGY #8 – WRITE YOUR GOALS DOWN ALONG WITH ACTION STEPS TO OBTAINING THEM

STRATEGY #9 – ESTABLISH A SCHEDULE TO WORK ON EACH ACTION STEP

TIME! IT IS one of the most precious gifts, yet it's mismanaged daily because people believe they will have more of it.

You have to learn how to value time and use it wisely. While there are 24 hours in a day, you have an opportunity to waste it if you allow distractions to steal your focus.

Establish a schedule to work on your goals and action steps. You will have to turn off the television, log off of social media, not respond to his/her text, say "NO" more often, etc. This will change some of your relationships because you'll start to see the dream killers come out, but you can either stay the same or work on creating the future you see for yourself.

This of course will require discipline! You can't stay up all night and expect to be well rested which is necessary for a productive day...notice I didn't say busy. You want to accomplish tasks, not run around unfocused and not complete anything. You must schedule EVERYTHING...I know that sounds a bit extreme, but I plan how long I'll need in the morning to prepare my breakfast, do my hair, put lotion on, pray, etc. Remember, time is ticking!

Tomorrow isn't promised...the next second isn't. Decide to do what's needed to diligently reach your finish line.

Write down your thoughts in the space provided. Here are some questions you may want to consider.

1. Are you tardy to everything? If so, why?

2. What are some hindrances to you staying on time?

3. Do you currently have a schedule you follow? If so, how is that working?

STRATEGY #9: ESTABLISH A SCHEDULE TO WORK ON EACH ACTION STEP

STRATEGY #10 – FIND A MENTOR

"MENTOR: MENTORSHIP IS a relationship in which a more experienced or more knowledgeable person helps to guide a less experienced or less knowledgeable person. The mentor may be older or younger than the person being mentored, but he or she must have a certain area of expertise." (Google/Wikipedia)

I believe everyone, at some point in their lives, needs to seek guidance from a mentor. I've had several in my life for business and personal goals. They are there to share wisdom, offer sound advice and hold you accountable. They are not your buddy or pal nor should you expect them to do your work. You must understand that you will be stretched in order to grow and it will be a bit uncomfortable (especially if this concept is new to you).

Do mentors work for free? Some do, yet others realize that their time is valuable as well as their knowledge and charge a fee. You'll have to decide how bad you want your life to change.

I do suggest you do your homework before hiring anyone, but don't get so picky that you forgo the process because of fear. In order to experience change, you have to shift gears...the speed you've been traveling at won't get you to the next level.

Now, you're probably thinking about that one cousin that you know who is a really great listener, but no! You can't get anyone to fulfill this position. You need a person who is successful in their life, focused, honest, etc. You need someone who will be real with you about your slackness...my life has definitely improved because I allowed my mentors to speak into my life!

Write down your thoughts in the space provided. Here are some questions you may want to consider.

1. Do you believe having a mentor is important? Why or why not?

2. What are some ways a mentor can help you achieve your goals?

3. Are you willing to pay someone to be your mentor? Why or why not?

____

____

____

____

____

____

____

____

____

____

____

____

____

STRATEGY #11 – WORK EVERY DAY ON YOUR GOALS

THIS IS THE one time I'll condone selfishness...yes, you will have to become laser focused to the point that you put yourself first on purpose!

Most people would say, they don't have a problem putting themselves first, but their life shows otherwise. Now, I'm not talking about being nasty, yet if it doesn't help you achieve your goals - you probably need to decline some invites...not answer some phone calls...tell your 16-year-old to look for their own sock...that type of thing.

You must set aside time everyday specifically for your goals. Notice, I didn't say how much time. Do what is appropriate for your schedule, but don't cheat yourself. While you're on social media for hours...use 1 of those hours to look up information needed to start that business, check into online colleges where you can finish up that degree, search listings in the area for homes you'd like to purchase one day - do something!

Make this step fun! Incorporate your friends, siblings, family...if you all are trying to achieve goals, why not make it a team effort. Have a vision board party, set up brainstorming meetings, discuss your goals daily - instead of talking about the latest tweet or who is seeing who - be about your business of manifesting your goals!

This strategy is for serious goal getters and it will challenge many of you, but I promise you'll start changing, you'll start seeing things differently – your vision will expand because you are now tapping deeper into faith understanding that it will take God to make things happen.

Write down your thoughts in the space provided. Here are some questions you may want to consider.

1. Do you find it hard to put yourself first? If so, why?

2. How important are your goals? What are you willing to sacrifice for them?

3. Do you have a support system in place? If so, who are they?

____

____

____

____

____

____

____

____

____

____

____

____

____

____

____

____

STRATEGY #12 – PRAY DAILY, BE OBEDIENT TO GOD AND STAY FOCUSED

I HOPE YOU enjoyed the 12 strategies and will use them to experience all of what God has for you and your family!

We started with establishing a relationship with God and we're closing with building upon that relationship. Prayer is such a beautiful gift because you have direct contact with your Heavenly Father. He's never busy and always ready to forgive you - when you repent. If prayer is new to you, simply consider it as talking to someone who knows EVERYTHING about you and still loves you madly!

God isn't a Father who looks to punish His children. Think about it - as parents you want to love, provide and protect your children. God is the same way, but to the 100,000 degree. He loves you and just wants you to be obedient as any parent would. However, when you fall short, repent! He eagerly awaits you and is rooting for you to get it right because He knows you have an amazing purpose/future.

I encourage you to take this moment to commit to staying focused on seeing God's plan for your life manifest. Most of the times you think your goals or visions come from you...sometimes, but I believe God plants the seed and wants you to be faithful to water that seed so it can grow.

Stay encouraged, keep God first and don't quit! You are on

your way and I'm praying for everyone who is working toward reaching their goal – you got this!

FAITH-BASED STRATEGIES TO PRODUCE MANIFESTATION OF YOUR GOALS

Write down your thoughts in the space provided. Here are some questions you may want to consider.

1. Do you currently pray? If so, when? If not, why?

2. What are some ways you replenish your spirit when you get weary?

3. What are some practical ways you can stay focused on your goals while building a stronger relationship with God?